Contents

Who ever sausage a thing?

One day a boy went walking,
And went into a store;
He bought a pound of sausages
And laid them on the floor.

The boy began to whistle
A merry little tune –
And all the little sausages
Danced around the room!

Anonymous

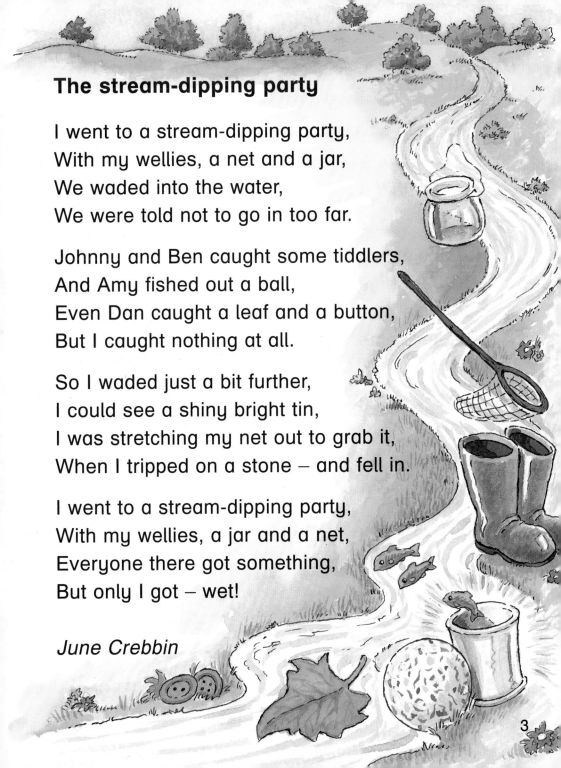

The stream-dipping party

I went to a stream-dipping party,
With my wellies, a net and a jar,
We waded into the water,
We were told not to go in too far.

Johnny and Ben caught some tiddlers,
And Amy fished out a ball,
Even Dan caught a leaf and a button,
But I caught nothing at all.

So I waded just a bit further,
I could see a shiny bright tin,
I was stretching my net out to grab it,
When I tripped on a stone – and fell in.

I went to a stream-dipping party,
With my wellies, a jar and a net,
Everyone there got something,
But only I got – wet!

June Crebbin

Fair Rosie

Fair Rosie was a lovely girl,
A lovely girl, a lovely girl,
Fair Rosie was a lovely girl,
A lovely girl.

Her ancient castle was her home,
Was her home, was her home,
Her ancient castle was her home,
Was her home.

Fair Rosie sat in her high tower,
Her high tower, her high tower,
Fair Rosie sat in her high tower,
Her high tower.

A wicked fairy found her there,
Found her there, found her there,
A wicked fairy found her there,
Found her there.

Fair Rosie slept a hundred years,
A hundred years, a hundred years,
Fair Rosie slept a hundred years,
A hundred years.

A handsome prince came riding by,
Riding by, riding by,
A handsome prince came riding by,
Riding by.

Fair Rosie she did sleep no more,
Sleep no more, sleep no more,
Fair Rosie she did sleep no more,
Sleep no more.

All the guests made merry there,
Merry there, merry there,
All the guests made merry there,
Merry there.

Anonymous

5

A mouse in the kitchen

There's a mouse in the kitchen
    Playing skittles with the peas,
He's drinking mugs of coffee
    And eating last week's cheese.

There's a mouse in the kitchen
    We could catch him in a hat,
Otherwise he'll toast the teacakes
    And that's bound to annoy the cat.

There's a mouse in the kitchen
    Ignoring all our wishes,
He's eaten tomorrow's dinner
    But at least he's washed the dishes.

John Rice

I had a little cat

I had a little cat called Tim Tom Tay,
I took him to town on market day,
I combed his whiskers, I brushed his tail,
I wrote on a label, "Cat for Sale.
Knows how to deal with rats and mice.
Two pounds fifty. Bargain price."

But when people came to buy
I saw such a look in Tim Tom's eye
That it was clear as clear could be
I couldn't sell Tim for a fortune's fee.
I was ashamed and sorry, I'll tell you plain,
And I took home Tim Tom Tay again.

Charles Causley

Cat for Sale
£2·50

7

There was an old lady
who swallowed a fly

There was an old lady who swallowed a fly.
I don't know why she swallowed a fly,
Perhaps she'll die.

There was an old lady who swallowed a spider
That wriggled and jiggled and tickled inside her.
She swallowed the spider to catch the fly,
I don't know why she swallowed the fly,
Perhaps she'll die.

There was an old lady who swallowed a bird.
How absurd to swallow a bird!
She swallowed the bird to catch the spider
That wriggled and jiggled and tickled inside her.
She swallowed the spider to catch the fly,
I don't know why she swallowed the fly,
Perhaps she'll die.

There was an old lady who swallowed a cat,
Imagine that, she swallowed a cat!
She swallowed the cat to catch the bird,
She swallowed the bird to catch the spider
That wriggled and jiggled and tickled inside her.
She swallowed the spider to catch the fly,
I don't know why she swallowed the fly,
Perhaps she'll die.

There was an old lady who swallowed a dog.
What a hog to swallow a dog!
She swallowed the dog to catch the cat,
She swallowed the cat to catch the bird,
She swallowed the bird to catch the spider
That wriggled and jiggled and tickled inside her.
She swallowed the spider to catch the fly,
I don't know why she swallowed the fly,
Perhaps she'll die.

There was an old lady who swallowed a goat.
Opened her throat and swallowed a goat!
She swallowed the goat to catch the dog,
She swallowed the dog to catch the cat,
She swallowed the cat to catch the bird,
She swallowed the bird to catch the spider
That wriggled and jiggled and tickled inside her.
She swallowed the spider to catch the fly,
I don't know why she swallowed the fly,
Perhaps she'll die.

There was an old lady who swallowed a cow.
I don't know how she swallowed a cow!
She swallowed the cow to catch the goat,
She swallowed the goat to catch the dog,
She swallowed the dog to catch the cat,
She swallowed the cat to catch the bird,
She swallowed the bird to catch the spider
That wriggled and jiggled and tickled inside her.

There was an old lady who swallowed a horse.
She's dead, of course!

Anonymous

The cure

"I've swallowed a fly," cried Marjorie Fry.
    (We could hear it buzzing inside her.)
"And I haven't a hope of getting it out
    Unless I swallow a spider."

We found a web by the garden wall,
    And back to the house we hurried
And offered the spider to Marjorie Fry,
    Who was looking extremely worried.

"Now shut your eyelids, Marjorie Fry,
    And open your wee mouth wider.
Whatever it does, the fly won't buzz
    If only you'll swallow the spider."

Alfred Noyes

11

There was an old lady

There was an old lady
    Whose kitchen was bare,
So she called for the cat
    Saying, "Time for some air!"

She sent him to buy her
    A packet of cheese
But the cat hurried back
    With a basket of bees.

She sent him to buy her
    A gallon of juice.
But the cat reappeared
    With a galloping goose.

She sent him to buy her
    A dinner of beef.
But the cat scampered home
    With an Indian chief.

She sent him to buy her
    A bowl of ice-cream.
But the cat skated in
    With a whole hockey team.

She sent him to buy her
    A bite of spaghetti.
But the cat strutted up
    With a bride and confetti.

She sent him to buy her
    A fine cup of tea.
But the cat waddled back
    With a dinosaur's knee.

The fridge was soon bulging,
    And so was the shelf.
So she sent for a hot dog
    And ate it herself.

Dennis Lee

The Owl and the Pussy-cat

The Owl and the Pussy-cat went to sea
    In a beautiful pea-green boat,
They took some honey and plenty of money,
    Wrapped up in a five-pound note.
The owl looked up to the stars above,
    And sang to a small guitar,
"O lovely Pussy! O Pussy, my love,
    What a beautiful Pussy you are,
            You are,
            You are!
What a beautiful Pussy you are!"

Pussy said to the Owl, "You elegant fowl!
    How charmingly sweet you sing!
O let us be married! Too long we have tarried;
    But what shall we do for a ring?"
They sailed away for a year and a day,
    To the land where the Bong-tree grows
And there in a wood a Piggy-wig stood
    With a ring at the end of his nose,
            His nose,
            His nose,
With a ring at the end of his nose.

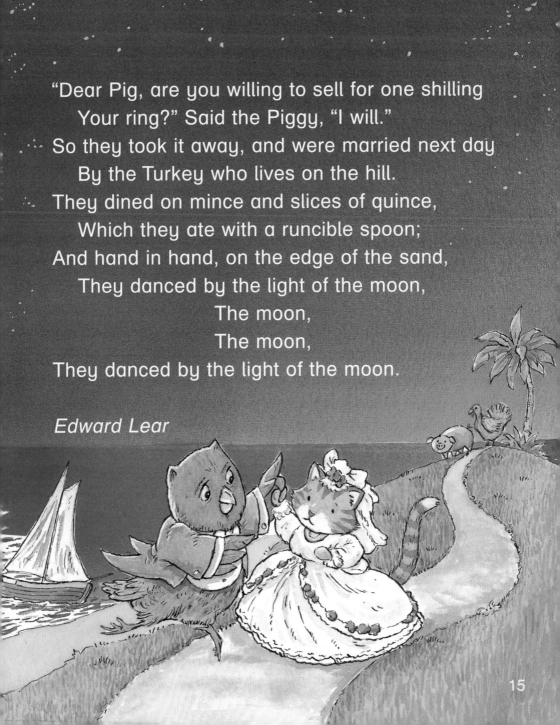

"Dear Pig, are you willing to sell for one shilling
    Your ring?" Said the Piggy, "I will."
So they took it away, and were married next day
    By the Turkey who lives on the hill.
They dined on mince and slices of quince,
    Which they ate with a runcible spoon;
And hand in hand, on the edge of the sand,
    They danced by the light of the moon,
                The moon,
                The moon,
They danced by the light of the moon.

Edward Lear

Anansi and the moon

Spiderman Anansi
went walking in the night.
Suddenly he noticed
a shining silver light.

He went to have a closer look,
and what was it he found?
A great big shiny silver pearl
lying on the ground.

"Ah!" cried Anansi.
"What a lovely sight!
I'll take it home to give my boys,
and fill them with delight."

But when Anansi showed it,
the boys could not agree.
They all began to argue, saying,
"Give it just to me!"

So, in the end, Anansi
threw it far and high.
It settled there among the stars,
floating in the sky.

And if you look at night-time
you'll see it hanging there:
a lovely round and silver moon
for all of us to share.

Tony Mitton

A strange morning

Strange things happened
when I woke today.
My shoes got up
and walked away.

And when I tried
to butter my bread
it turned
and buttered me instead.

A voice from the teapot
began to speak:
"Don't pour me yet,
I'm much too weak!"

The cat keeps sitting
on my head.
I think I'll just
go back to bed!

Irene Rawnsley

Windy nights

Whenever the moon and stars are set,
Whenever the wind is high,
All night long in the dark and wet,
A man goes riding by.
Late in the night when the fires are out,
Why does he gallop and gallop about?

Whenever the trees are crying aloud,
And ships are tossed at sea,
By, on the highway, low and loud,
By at the gallop goes he.
By at the gallop he goes, and then
By he comes back at the gallop again.

Robert Louis Stevenson

19

Best day

"This is the best day of my life,"
said Jimmy to the school secretary.

"Oh, yes," she said. "Why's that?"
"I'm being sent home," he said.
"Oh, dear," she said. "Why's that?"

"Spots," he said. "All over."

And he showed her.

June Crebbin

Sad Sidney

Sad Sidney buttered a tea-cake
And buttered cream-crackers galore
And buttered his chair and the hearth-rug
And buttered across to the door.

Sad Sidney buttered the gatepost
And buttered the kerb of the street
And buttered along to the bus stop
And buttered upstairs to a seat.

Sad Sidney buttered the depot
And buttered his way out of sight
And buttered the road to Portsmouth
And buttered the Isle of Wight.

Sad Sidney buttered the beaches
And buttered right up to the tide,
Then, finding his butter dish empty,
Sat down on the pebbles and cried.

Richard Edwards

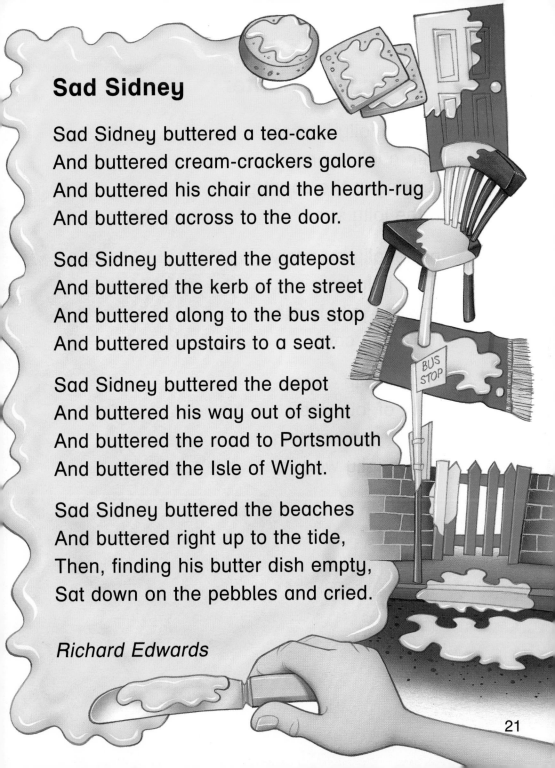

I saw a jolly hunter

I saw a jolly hunter
With a jolly gun
Walking in the country
In the jolly sun.

In the jolly meadow
Sat a jolly hare.
Saw the jolly hunter
Took jolly care.

Hunter jolly eager –
Sight of jolly prey.
Forgot gun pointing
Wrong jolly way.

Jolly hunter jolly head
Over heels gone.
Jolly old safety-catch
Not jolly on.

Bang went the jolly gun.
Hunter jolly dead.
Jolly hare got clean away
Jolly good I said.

Charles Causley

A good play

We built a ship upon the stairs
All made of the back bedroom chairs,
And filled it full of sofa pillows
To go a-sailing on the billows.

We took a saw and several nails,
And water in nursery pails;
And Tom said, "Let us also take
An apple and a slice of cake",
Which was enough for Tom and me
To go a-sailing on, till tea.

We sailed along for days and days,
And had the very best of plays,
But Tom fell out and hurt his knee,
So there was no one left but me.

Robert Louis Stevenson